AF488059

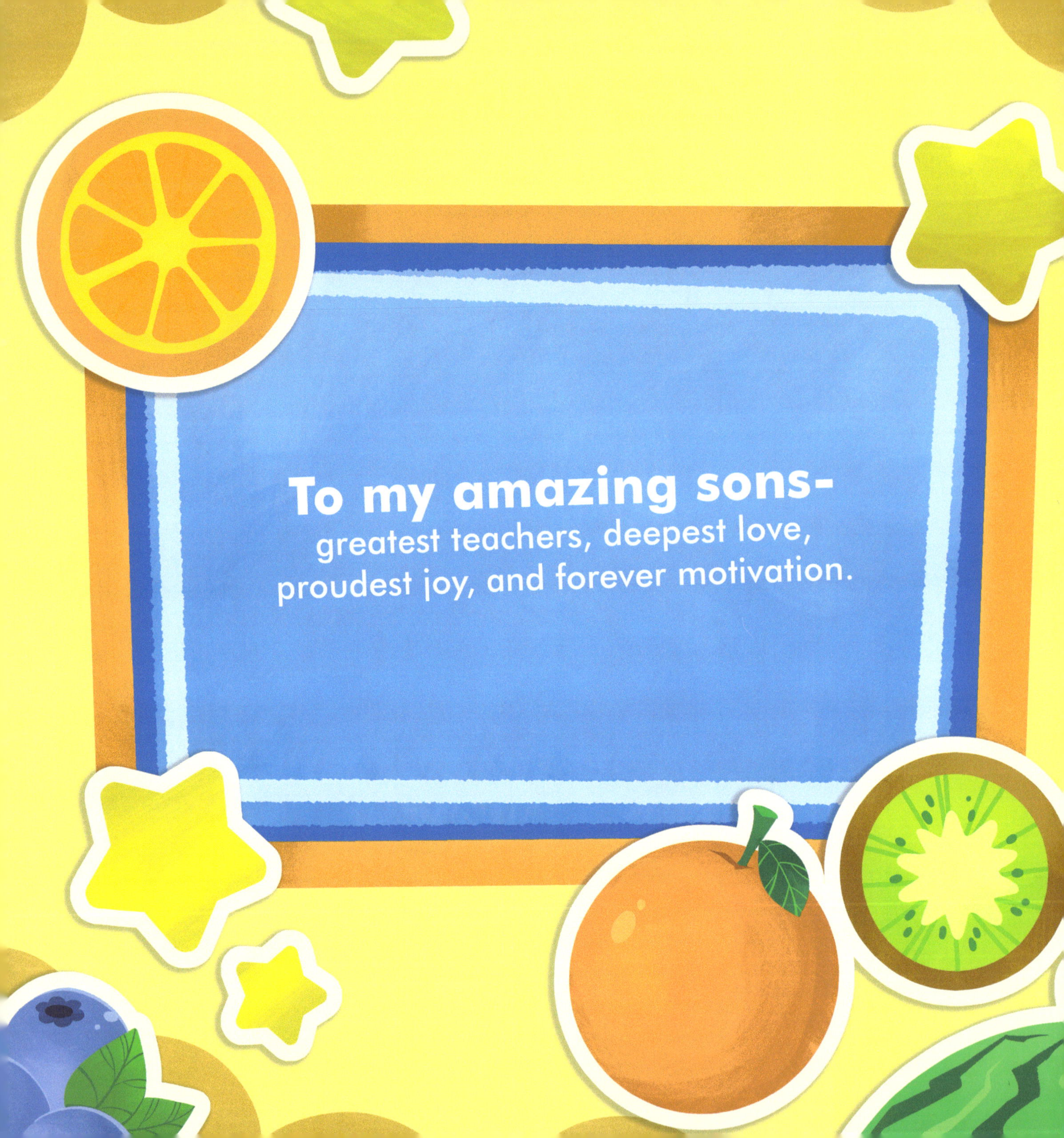To my amazing sons-
greatest teachers, deepest love,
proudest joy, and forever motivation.

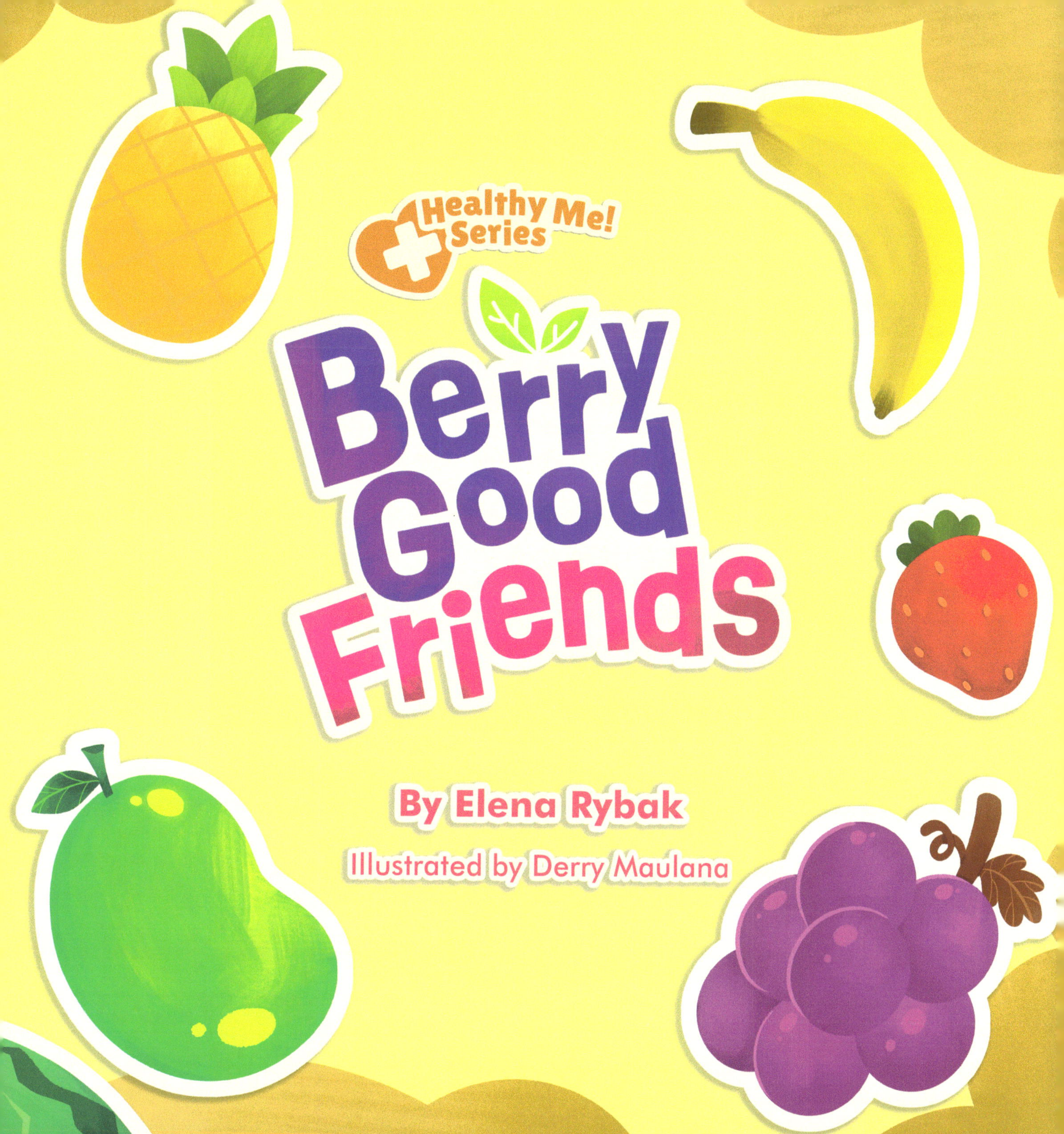

Healthy Me! Series
Berry Good Friends
By Elena Rybak
Illustrated by Derry Maulana

Red, green, yellow, pink—
What's your favorite fruit, you think?

Apples crunch with every bite,
Help your teeth stay clean and bright.

Bananas bend, they like to play,
Give you energy all day!

HA HA
HA HA

Oranges giggle, round and sweet,
Vitamin C from head to feet.

Blueberries bounce, they roll, they pop,
Brainy power—nonstop, nonstop!

Strawberries wear their hats of green,
Keep your tummy strong and clean.

Grapes hold hands in tiny bunch,
Heart-happy snacks for school or lunch.

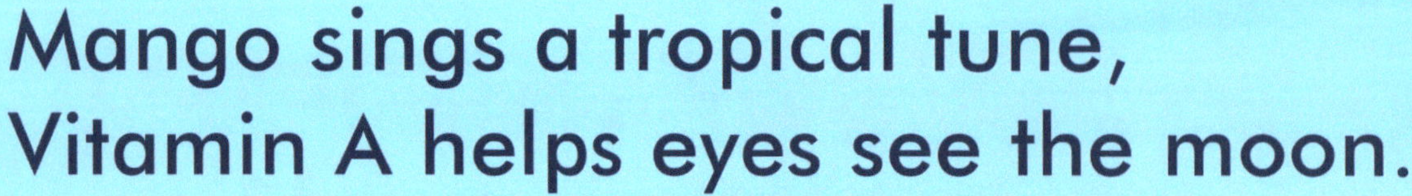

Mango sings a tropical tune,
Vitamin A helps eyes see the moon.

Pineapple prickly, tall, and proud,
Heals your body—shout it loud!

Watermelon juicy, cool, and bright,
Keeps you hydrated day and night.

Kiwi fuzzy, green inside,
Strength and power in every bite!

So many colors, shapes, and sizes,
Fruit brings health and sweet surprises!

Parent Tips

Offer fruit in fun ways: cut into shapes, make fruit kabobs, or blend smoothies.

Encourage kids to "eat the rainbow" by choosing different colors each day.

Let your child help pick fruit at the store or farmer's market—they're more likely to try it.

Pair fruit with protein (like yogurt or nuts) for a longer-lasting snack.